Your Security
Details

Dr. Michael Andam

Your Security
Details

KDP

Your Security Details.
© 2020 Dr. Michael Andam

Published by KDP

Cover. Art work of Special agents drawn by author.

Dedicated to

All followers of Jesus

Content.

Preface

This material is part of my journey as a child of God. Reflecting on the first time I came to accept Jesus as both my Saviour and asked Him to lead me as Lord, many challenging things have happened till date.

One of the significant aspects of making a conscious decision of living for Christ till your last day is that, the devil will do all he can to attack this decision with all forms of lies and false accusations in an attempt to destroy that relationship with Christ and confidence in Him.

There are some circles that teach this false doctrine such as once you come to Christ, all your problems go away and you will not have problems. This is not true to an extent. On the other hand, I have come to understand that the Biblical doctrines are true. Once you come to follow Christ, there will be many afflictions that come your way. No matter how painful these are God is indeed able to deliver you from it all.

One of the main reasons for this material on top of these reasons for our protection is that some in the Christian circle think that the closer you get to God the stronger the demons assigned to you. This philosophy is almost an invitation to not desire to get too close to God.

This is in contrast to what God said and encourages us to do. He said we should draw close to Him and He will draw close to us. We could then resist the devil who will flee from us. I used the examples God uses to protect all His children to explain that the higher and closer we are to God the higher and stronger our protection from God. I hope this material together with reading of the Bible will encourage you to get closer to God each day.

Introduction

The first chapter introduces us to the world of security of important personalities who by the virtue of their position and leadership need to be protected. This is compared to how God protects His children.

Chapter two focuses on security of God's children, which is more powerful than that which the world can offer.

The third chapter highlights the executive knowledge of intentional protection of God's people using a typical example of that of the biblical personality, Job.

Chapter four teaches on the unique way of how God protects His children.

Chapter five discusses how those given higher assignment by God are protected to accomplish such tasks.

Chapter six discloses God's unlimited resources when it comes to the protecting of His children.

Chapter seven reveals Jesus' security details from birth through to His ministry period.

Chapter eight looks at the apostles Peter's security details as he carried out the leadership role in leading the early church.

The final chapter is open for us to understand our security details and the confidence we can have in following and doing the will of Christ.

❖Chapter one
The General's Security details

Who is protected most?

Have you heard the statement the higher you go with God the stronger the Demons? Seems pretty logical. This concept almost sounds convincing and true. Unfortunately it could also have the capacity to cause many Christians to avoid becoming stronger by and getting closer to God to avoid having stronger demons to contend with.

We may be experiencing enough trials and temptations already due to our present relationship with God. We may like to stay in this kind of comfort zone with not much serious attacks. Well, anything that prevents people from getting into a closer relationship with Jesus Christ is not from God but a suggestion from the devil just as always.

The book of James encourages us to draw close to God and He will in turn draw close to us. "Draw near to God and He will draw near to you. Cleanse your hands, you sinners; and purify your hearts, you double-minded." - James 4:8. It is the will of God to get close to Him. Anything that has to do with the will of God has God's undivided attention. Any other that is contrary to His will as revealed in His word will not attract God's attention.

Ground rules of security

Let's put these cards on the table right away. The security agents that are assigned to be with presidents and those public figures needing protection are there to make their presence known to them. It is to say we will be with you wherever you go. Individuals would sound like "I will be with you, Mr./Madam president."

God protects His children in the most powerful way too. His standard is in what He says to them: "I will be with you." We might be aware of this or have no idea or awareness of this for whatsoever. It doesn't matter as God still protects His children and does not need our permission to do so. That is the highest level of protection anyone can get on earth! To have the presence of the Creator of the whole universe is the only highest level of protection we should all desire to have and be aware of.

"Fear not, for I am with you; be not dismayed, for I am your God. I will strengthen you, Yes, I will help you, I will uphold you with My righteous right hand.'"-Isaiah 41:10. What assuring powerful words of truth. God speaks His word and do exactly as He intends.

Lets consider the Security detail for a president and cabinet ministers. Taking the presidency of the United States and other countries that follow similar structures, the protection of the president and Vice President are mandatory. They have classified full security details, meaning heavily protected by their countries secret services. Secret service special agents give 24-hour protection for the president and Vice President and their immediate families.

Currently there are about three thousand two hundred special agents with an additional thousand three hundred uniformed agents who guard the White House and other high profile buildings in the United States of America. Other countries that follow this system have similar or even more security personnel protecting the presidency and the others.

The higher up the power hierarchy you go, the more you are protected due to the heightened potential level of attacks due to the level of importance. I believe we have all seen the president or leaders of our countries' motorcade and the highest level of security wherever they go. Many now have their own presidential planes and helicopters that make protecting them effective.

Many a time you may not see all the security agents protecting the president. Let there be any form of threat and you will see the details spring into action and forming a protective shield around the president. They will normally whisk the President away into their secured motorcade and speed off away from harm. The others will stay and try to neutralize the situation.

The United Kingdom's royal family members are also protected with personal armed bodyguards at all times. Every visit is scrutinised and checked to ensure each member have security as they carry out their royal duties. They are heavily protected. For example, they are not allowed to close the doors of their chauffeured cars for security reasons as the cars are self-locking etc.

I believe every leader of a country nowadays have their security details especially in these times.

Why security for leaders?

Leaders are like captains of a ship. They are the ones steering the ship to its designated destination. Loosing the captain in the middle of a storm would not be a good experience for those on board the ship. The same reason army generals are protected by number of soldiers.

In the United States of America, the secret service was originally formed to combat widespread criminal acts of currency counterfeiting. From its inception from 1865 to 3003, it came under the US treasury department. From 2003 to present, it is under the US homeland security. Their core objectives are to protect and to investigate.

Among many other high profile security investigations such as analysing handwriting, one of their primary missions now is to protect the nation's highest elected leaders and other high-ranking government officials. This mission was enacted after the assassination of President William McKinley in 1901. Congress directed the secret services to protect the president of the United States. It became a law to protect the president. Also, the Vice President and those in succession should the need arise. There is a whole list of them.

The president, vice president (or other officer next in the order of succession to the Office of President, should the vice presidency be vacant),
President-elect and vice president---elect.
The immediate families of the above individuals and few more.

The point is that the secret service does not protect the whole country. It protect the president who is the highest elected leader and thus subject to more dangers than the average citizen. This is why the security details are classified otherwise what would be the point of it?

There will forever be those who are always planning attacks on high-ranking officials for so many reasons. The constant plotting to harm leaders due to many reasons they have will continue to put the secret service agents on high alert at all times to protect them.

Summary
- This will be the foundation we can build on meaning the closer you get to God, the more the devil targets and desires to attack and destroy you.
- The closer you get to a God the stronger your security and protection.
- You have the highest level of protection on earth. God is with you.

Chapter Two

Security details for God's children

Permanent presence

God said I will be with you. Our security details are linked to the calling and purposes for our lives. I will be with you to accomplish what I have called you to be and that is the highest form of protection. This is the highest level of protection we can ever have. If the King and creator of everything spiritual and natural promises to be with you then who else can give you anything higher?

Jacob, the grandson of Abraham was traveling towards a place called Haran. He came to a place and chose to pass the night. He used one of the stones as a pillow to sleep on. While sleeping on this stone pillow he had a dream. "Then he dreamed, and behold, a ladder was set up on the earth, and its top reached to heaven; and there the angels of God were ascending and descending on it. And behold, the LORD stood above it and said: "I am the LORD God of Abraham your father and the God of Isaac; the land on which you lie I will give to you and your descendants. Also your descendants shall be as the dust of the earth; you shall spread abroad to the west and the east, to the north and the south; and in you and in your seed all the families of the earth shall be blessed."-Genesis 28:12-14.

God just confirmed to him promises made to Abraham to be established through the covenant child Isaac, his father. God was now walking him into greatness, which meant the attacks from Satan will be great as well. Here is what God said He will do to protect him. This is for all of us who can call God our Father: "Behold, I am with you and will keep you wherever you go, and will bring you back to this land; for I will not leave you until I have done what I have spoken to you.""-Genesis 28:15.

This is our everlasting assurance of God's presence with us and the absolute protection that comes with it. Whatever impossible promises God has for you will come to pass in His own time as He never default on His word.

This is what happened: When God utters a word, that word is part of Him as He is the word and that word is part of God's overall plan. This is the reason He watches over all His word to perform it. Whatever He says is established. He spoke to the prophet Jeremiah asking him what he saw? The prophet said an almond tree. This was the lord's answer "Then the LORD said to me, "You have seen well, for I am ready to perform My word.""-Jeremiah 1:12.

Coming back to Jacob's story. Jacob woke up from this wonderful vision and immediately acknowledged the presence of God in that place. "Then Jacob awoke from his sleep and said, "Surely the LORD is in this place, and I did not know it. " And he was afraid and said, "How awesome is this place! This is none other than the house of God, and this is the gate of heaven!"...Then Jacob made a vow, saying, "If God will be with me, and keep me in this way that I am going, and give me bread to eat and clothing to put on, so that I come back to my father's house in peace, then the LORD shall be my God."- Genesis 28:16-17, 20-21. It was not because he did not believe in God. On the other hand they had a knack for making covenants. "And this stone which I have set as a pillar shall be God's house, and of all that You give me I will surely give a tenth to You.""- Genesis 28:22. It was mainly a sense of awe and reverence for God's presence and revelation of promises at an unexpected place.

Summary

- God will reveal Himself to you as He chooses to reassure you of His presence, purpose for you and how He will protect you until this word is fulfilled.
- We can acknowledge the presence of God when He reveals Himself to us.
- God watches over His word and performs it according to His power.

❖**Chapter Three**
Executive evidence of protection

Highest security details

Many may or may not be familiar with the story of a man called Job in the Bible. We will look at a revelation that helps us understand this concept of our protection from God. Before we can get to this revelation, let's first get this man's background and how that related to this revelation of what I compare to security details.

There have been much research into who Job was and the time he lived. One of the people mentioned in his story in the book of job called Eliphaz, connects others from Jacob's genealogy from one school of thought. He was described as a comforter to Job (Job2: 11).

One school of thought traces Job's genealogy to that of Jacob, Abraham's grandson. The first time the name is mentioned was when the family of Jacob was invited to live in Egypt by Pharaoh because of Joseph who had been made second in command to Pharaoh. At the time God encouraged Jacob to accept pharaohs' invitation as He promised to be with him. "So He said, "I am God, the God of your father; do not fear to go down to Egypt, for I will make of you a great nation there."-Genesis 46:3.

"Now these were the names of the children of Israel, Jacob and his sons, who went to Egypt: Reuben was Jacob's firstborn.... The sons of Issachar were Tola, Puvah, Job, and Shimron."-Genesis 46:8, 13. Jacob had a twin brother called Esau. Let's look at the immediate genealogy of Abraham: "And Abraham begot Isaac. The sons of Isaac were Esau and Israel. The sons of Esau were Eliphaz, Reuel, Jeush, Jaalam, and Korah."-I Chronicles 1:34-35. (God changed Jacob's name to Israel)

During Job's story, Eliphaz was presented as one of his friends. However he spoke and said he knew Job's father who he was older than he. "What do you know that we do not know? What do you understand that is not in us? Both the gray-haired and the aged are among us, Much older than your father."-Job 15:9-10. It is said that Essau married earlier than Jacob. Essau married at the age of forty while Jacob (Israel) at the age of seventy. "When Esau was forty years old, he took as wives Judith the daughter of Beeri the Hittite, and Basemath the daughter of Elon the Hittite."-Genesis 26:34. If Eliphaz said he was older than Job that will be true as Essau's children were older than Jacob's.

From this account, we can conclude that Job was among the seventy souls who were descendants of Jacob (Israel) who moved to Egypt.

However, other scholars have concluded that the Job mentioned in the book of Job is different from the one mentioned in the Genesis account using Hebrew text and others. Whichever is right, there is something to learn from his story for the purpose of this study. This man was real and not a myth.

Now let's look at Jobs family and the purpose for the study in this chapter:
Name: Job
Address: The land of Uz
Status: Blameless and upright and one who feared God and shunned evil.
Family: Wife, Seven sons three daughters.
Breakdown of wealth
Sheep: 7,000
Camel: 3,000
Yoke of oxen: 5,000
Female donkeys: 500
Household workers: Very large
Community standing: Greatest of all the people from the East.
This was quite impressive! He was the richest and greatest in the land.

Life in the job family:
It is recorded that the sons organised parties on their appointed days and invited their three sisters to celebrate with them. Jobs' fear of God made him to practice intercession for his children in case they committed sin during their celebration. "So it was, when the days of feasting had run their course, that

Job would send and sanctify them, and he would rise early in the morning and offer burnt offerings according to the number of them all. For Job said, "It may be that my sons have sinned and cursed God in their hearts." Thus Job did regularly."-Job 1:5.

Heaven

Meanwhile somewhere in God Almighty's seat of total power and reign, something unusual was happening. It was recorded that there was a day when the angels presented themselves before the Lord in heaven. This could be an occasion or anything on heaven's agenda we must not necessarily understand until we get there. "Now there was a day when the sons of God came to present themselves before the LORD, and Satan also came among them."-Job 1:6. Notice that Satan came too and was immediately spotted by God. God questioned and had a chat with him as follow: (scripture from Job 1:7-12)

God: "... "From where do you come?"
Satan:..."From going to and fro on the earth, and from walking back and forth on it."
God: ... "Have you considered My servant Job, that there is none like him on the earth, a blameless and upright man, one who fears God and shuns evil?"
Satan: ..."Does Job fear God for nothing? Have You not made a hedge around him, around his household, and around all that he has on every side?

You have blessed the work of his hands, and his possessions have increased in the land."-Job 1:9-10 . Satan: "But now, stretch out Your hand and touch all that he has, and he will surely curse You to Your face!""-Job 1:11.

Analysis of Jobs Security details: The conversation in heaven reveals how God protects His children who fear and live upright for Him. Satan could not penetrate through Job's security details. This was in his own words. This is incredible and a vital piece of information for us. He said God had made a hedge not just around Job but everyone and everything that belongs to him. This conversation was going on in heaven. For God to ask and boast about Job meant He knew Satan had tried to 'break' or penetrate through the hedge of protection to destroy Job but couldn't. It is amazing to know from here that Satan is aware of how well protected we are by our Father in heaven.

The second part of the conversation should reassure us that God never leaves nor forsake us. Majority of the terrible afflictions we face and go through happen as a matter of God boasting to Satan about how we fear Him! The point here is that Satan is not god and cannot penetrate or break God's protocol without God's permission. You heard from his own mouth. We should take a second and thank God for this fact.

It happened to Job without him knowing. From the last scripture Satan accused Job of serving

Him because of the blessings and protection. Satan suggested that if that were taken off, Job would cease to worship God. Now see what happened to his security details:

"And the LORD said to Satan, "Behold, all that he has is in your power; only do not lay a hand on his person. " So Satan went out from the presence of the LORD."-Job 1:12. Satan went out immediately and destroyed everything that Job had including killing all his children! This is the kind of invisible enemy we are dealing with. The good news is that, God is still with you and nothing takes Him by surprise.

During the rapid series of destruction, Satan spared one servant to come and report the calamity to Job. ..."While he was still speaking, another also came and said, "Your sons and daughters were eating and drinking wine in their oldest brother's house, and suddenly a great wind came from across the wilderness and struck the four corners of the house, and it fell on the young people, and they are dead; and I alone have escaped to tell you!" Then Job arose, tore his robe, and shaved his head; and he fell to the ground and worshiped....In all this Job did not sin nor charge God with wrong."-Job 1:18-20. Job did not give up on God. This infuriated Satan and he went to God and asked for more access to Job.

Heaven
There was another occasion just as the first one and Satan also came with the angels. God asked him the same questions as before concerning Job. This time

he pointed out how Satan incited God to destroy him without cause. When you face a sudden attack that doesn't make sense remember it is not because you have done anything wrong but God boasted about you and Satan was allowed to cause destruction for a short season.

God: "Then the LORD said to Satan, "Have you considered My servant Job, that there is none like him on the earth, a blameless and upright man, one who fears God and shuns evil? And still he holds fast to his integrity, although you incited Me against him, to destroy him without cause.""-Job 2:3. Satan had another destructive agenda planned as always.

Satan: "So Satan answered the LORD and said, "Skin for skin! Yes, all that a man has he will give for his life. But stretch out Your hand now, and touch his bone and his flesh, and he will surely curse You to Your face!""-Job 2:4-5.

God: "And the LORD said to Satan, "Behold, he is in your hand, but spare his life.""-Job 2:6.

God removed all of Job's protection apart from his life. There are times we will go through some serious health issues, which may be as a result of the same reason Job went through. Just see how swift Satan moves once he knew the protection was off. "So Satan went out from the presence of the LORD, and struck Job with painful boils from the sole of his foot to the crown of his head."-Job 2:7.

At the end of this satanic influenced ordeal, God blessed Job's latter days more than in the beginning. "And the LORD restored Job's losses when he prayed for his friends. Indeed the LORD gave Job twice as much as he had before.

Now the LORD blessed the latter days of Job more than his beginning; for he had fourteen thousand sheep, six thousand camels, one thousand yoke of oxen, and one thousand female donkeys. He also had seven sons and three daughters. And he called the name of the first Jemimah, the name of the second Keziah, and the name of the third Keren-Happuch."-Job 42:10, 12-14.

Summary

- The first time we got a clear picture of God's strong security detail for job was when Satan voiced out his frustration of not been able to penetrate through! It was a fortress!

- God acknowledged that He had completed protected Job and all he had.

- Notice that Job chose to fear God and worshipped him faithfully.

- He had no idea of what went on in heaven that was to cause him all he had on earth.

- He would have been in shock with the sudden rapid loss of all within that short period of time. It did not make sense as this was spiritually orchestrated with God's permission.

- Although everyone and everything job had was stripped away bare, Job realised he had God and nothing or no one could take Him away from him.

- Satan was put to shame, as God was right about Job. He did not serve God because of the blessings from God.

- Although Job's had the scares of the lost of his children, God was still glorified and pleases with him.

Chapter Four

God protects His children

Pre Security checks

Before the president travels anywhere, the security forces travels ahead of time to ensure the place is safe before the arrival of the president. The time the secret service go and secure such places may depend on how safe or dangerous they classify the place. Once they are there, they ensure the place is totally secured in all areas. They plan to cover and secure every possible eventuality and what to do in possible security breaches. The most important factor is that they always plan ahead.

God's children have a more powerful and impressive security details with a more and better sophisticated advanced pre checks. The bottom line is that God protects His children in a very powerful and unique way. "For whom He foreknew, He also predestined to be conformed to the image of His Son, that He might be the firstborn among many brethren. Moreover whom He predestined, these He also called; whom He called, these He also justified; and whom He justified, these He also glorified."- Romans 8:29-30.

God knows our end from the beginning and nothing surprises Him. He is able to protect us wherever we find ourselves. God knows where we will be and hence our security details are planned in advance. Nothing escapes Gods mind and plan.

King David's security details

Undoubtedly God was so pleased with David and called him a man after His heart. God chose him to be king over his people Israel, at the time.

One thing we need to understand is that God's angels involved in our protection and our security details are classified. The fact that you do not see them does not imply nonexistent. The angels are at work always protecting us from the evil one.

Before David was chosen by God and anointed as King, the first king of Israel, Saul, was already reigning. The disobedience of king Saul saw his kingdom brought to an end. Before David was anointed as king, he was a shepherd looking after the family flock of sheep as the youngest member of the family.

This was what God said about him to the prophet who was to carry out God's instructions in anointing him as king. "But now your kingdom shall not continue. The LORD has sought for Himself a man after His own heart, and the LORD has commanded him to be commander over His people, because you have not kept what the LORD commanded you.""-I Samuel 13:14.

God stopped Saul's kingdom and established David's even before he knew about it. Look at the words God used. The Lord has made him commander over his people including his army. David did not have a clue what God had said about him.

There was pure drama when the prophet Samuel went to the house of Jesse, David's dad, to anoint one of his sons as God directed. On arrival and explanation on his purpose, the sons of Jesse were presented before the prophet from Eliab, the eldest to the last but one. When Samuel saw Eliab's physical stature he believed God's chosen anointed was right before him! "So it was, when they came, that he looked at Eliab and said, "Surely the LORD's anointed is before Him!" But the LORD said to Samuel, "Do not look at his appearance or at his physical stature, because I have refused him. For the LORD does not see as man sees; for man looks at the outward appearance, but the LORD looks at the heart.""-I Samuel 16:6-7.

All seven sons presented before the prophet in God's presence were not chosen. Samuel may have thought what was going on? Are these all your sons Jesse, as God had chosen none? The dad now remembered the youngest who was looking after the sheep. They were not to sit until he was brought in.

"So he sent and brought him in. Now he was ruddy, with bright eyes, and good-looking. And the LORD said, "Arise, anoint him; for this is the one!" Then Samuel took the horn of oil and anointed him in the midst of his brothers; and the Spirit of the LORD came upon David from that day forward. So Samuel arose and went to Ramah."-I Samuel 16:12-13.

After he was anointed as king, he was to stand by until Saul's kingdom came to an end. One day he was sent by his dad to send items to his brothers who were in Saul's army preparing to fight the philistines. On his arrival, he saw this giant of a man blaspheming against his God and defying the army of God. Remember the Holy Spirit of the Lord came over him from that day forward.

He heard the blasphemy and said he will fight this giant. He was brought to the king. This is what he said to him: "Then David said to Saul, "Let no man's heart fail because of him; your servant will go and fight with this Philistine.""-I Samuel 17:32. When he was brought to the king for volunteering to fight, the king discouraged him as he was a youth compared to Goliath who was a seasoned warrior. "And Saul said to David, "You are not able to go against this Philistine to fight with him; for you are a youth, and he a man of war from his youth.""-I Samuel 17:33.

David knew how protected he was. "But David said to Saul, "Your servant used to keep his father's sheep, and when a lion or a bear came and took a lamb out of the flock, I went out after it and struck it, and delivered the lamb from its mouth; and when it arose against me, I caught it by its beard, and struck and killed it. Your servant has killed both lion and bear; and this uncircumcised Philistine will be like one of them, seeing he has defied the armies of the living God." Moreover David said, "The LORD, who delivered me from the paw of the lion and from the paw of the bear, He will deliver me from the hand of this Philistine." And Saul said to David, "Go, and the LORD be with you!""-I Samuel 17:34-37.

Apart from king David having mighty men of valour ready to protect him, God first and foremost protected him. He knew his security details were from God. David made this clear in many of his poems compiled as part of the book of psalms in the Bible. One of such is psalm 23. Using his previous career as a shepherd, he attributes the ultimate protective and caring nature of God as the Shepherd. "The LORD is my shepherd; I shall not want....Yea, though I walk through the valley of the shadow of death, I will fear no evil; For You are with me; Your rod and Your staff, they comfort me."-Psalms 23:1, 4.

We should remember that in David's time the threats were both spiritual and mainly physical from either a spiritual or a real physical enemy army. This is another of David's psalms: "The LORD is my light and my salvation; Whom shall I fear? The LORD is the strength of my life; Of whom shall I be afraid? When the wicked came against me to eat up my flesh, My enemies and foes, They stumbled and fell. Though an army may encamp against me, My heart shall not fear; Though war may rise against me, In this I will be confident....For in the time of trouble He shall hide me in His pavilion; In the secret place of His tabernacle He shall hide me; He shall set me high upon a rock."-Psalms 27:1-3, 5. David was fully confident of his divine security details.

David described how the topography of Jerusalem is and compares that to the everlasting protection from the Father. "Those who trust in the LORD are like Mount Zion, which cannot be moved, but abides forever. As the mountains surround Jerusalem, so the LORD surrounds His people From this time forth and forever."-Psalms 125:1-2. David was explaining to us the inexhaustible ways God surrounds us with His continual care and protection.

There is another instance among many when David revealed how God surrounds His children with His protection. "The angel of the LORD encamps all around those who fear Him, and delivers them."-Psalms 34:7. As the secret service Agents have their eyes fixed on the ones they protect, so is God's eyes fixed on His children. He also hears their cry for help. "The eyes of the LORD are on the righteous, And His ears are open to their cry."-Psalms 34:15.
"He shall cover you with His feathers, and under His wings you shall take refuge; His truth shall be your shield and buckler. You shall not be afraid of the terror by night, nor of the arrow that flies by day,"-Psalms 91:4-5.

Robust security details
"A thousand may fall at your side, and ten thousand at your right hand; But it shall not come near you. Only with your eyes shall you look, and see the reward of the wicked. Because you have made the LORD, who is my refuge, even the Most High, your dwelling place, no evil shall befall you, nor shall any

plague come near your dwelling; For He shall give His angels charge over you, to keep you in all your ways. In their hands they shall bear you up, lest you dash your foot against a stone."-Psalms 91:7-12.

Summary

- God predestines and provide protection ahead of time for His children.
- God's protection and care surrounds us just like the mountains surrounds Jerusalem.
- We are not to be afraid of any enemy.
- Because of God's powerful protection no evil shall befall you.

Chapter Five

Higher assignment- higher divine protection

Promise of protection

Baby Moses' security details.

Moses was born in Egypt at the time when the current Pharaoh was scared of the rate at which the Hebrew population was growing in his country. He was scared that they would join the nation's enemies should war broke out. Out of fear He ordered the murder of all Hebrew baby boys. That was why Moses' mum hatched a plan to safe her precious beautiful baby boy.

"And a man of the house of Levi went and took as wife a daughter of Levi. So the woman conceived and bore a son. And when she saw that he was a beautiful child, she hid him three months. But when she could no longer hide him, she took an ark of bulrushes for him, daubed it with asphalt and pitch, put the child in it, and laid it in the reeds by the river's bank. And his sister stood afar off, to know what would be done to him."-Exodus 2:1-4

Moses ended up in the house of Pharaoh as his daughter found the baby in that watertight basket on the river Nile where she visited. "Then the daughter of Pharaoh came down to bathe at the river. And her maidens walked along the riverside; and when she saw the ark among the reeds, she sent her maid to get it. And when she opened it, she saw the child, and behold, the baby wept. So she had compassion on him, and said, "This is one of the Hebrews' children." Then his sister said to Pharaoh's daughter, "Shall I go and call a nurse for you from the Hebrew women, that she may nurse the child for you?" And Pharaoh's daughter said to her, "Go." So the maiden went and called the child's mother. Then Pharaoh's daughter said to her, "Take this child away and nurse him for me, and I will give you your wages." So the woman took the child and nursed him. And the child grew, and she brought him to Pharaoh's daughter, and he became her son. So she called his name Moses, saying, "Because I drew him out of the water.""-Exodus 2:5-10.

When Moses grew up, He came to know of his roots. His people were made slaves. He once visited and saw an Egyptian beating a Hebrew, one of his brethren. "So he looked this way and that way, and when he saw no one, he killed the Egyptian and hid him in the sand."-Exodus 2:12. He went back the next day and found two of his brethren fighting. He confronted the one at fault. They made him aware that his secret was out: "Then he said, "Who made you a prince and a judge over us? Do you intend "to kill me as you killed the Egyptian?" So Moses feared and said, "Surely this thing is known!""-Exodus 2:14. Moses had to go into exile.

God knew the baby Moses before he was even conceived and planned out a purpose for him to deliver Israel from bondage in Egypt. That was part of his security details to be preserved, found and live to be trained as a prince at the palace. He was now ready for godly training as a shepherd of God's people. He was first to look after sheep for his father in law for forty years. God protected him all those years until He officially called and revealed Himself as God to him.

Calling and security details

During a normal days routine of taking the sheep out for pasture, Moses was to have an extraordinary and supernatural experience with the Creator God. On reaching around what was called the mountain of God, an angel appeared to Him in a spectacular way that immediately attracted Moses' attention to draw near and investigate. "And the Angel of the LORD appeared to him in a flame of fire from the midst of a bush. So he looked, and behold, the bush was burning with fire, but the bush was not consumed."-Exodus 3:2.

God asked him not to turn aside to look as He was standing on Holy grounds. God introduced Himself to Moses directly as that had not yet happened. "So when the LORD saw that he turned aside to look, God called to him from the midst of the bush and said, "Moses, Moses!" And he said, "Here I am." Then He said, "Do not draw near this place. Take your sandals off your feet, for the place where you stand is holy ground." Moreover He said, "I am the God of your father—the God of Abraham, the God of Isaac, and the God of Jacob." And Moses hid his face, for he was afraid to look upon God."-Exodus 3:4-6.

God gave him the assignment of meeting with Pharaoh and asking him to let the children of Israel get out of Egypt unto a land God has chosen for them. From this interaction, Moses got closer to God as time went on. Let's see Moses' natural reaction and God making known how He was going to protect him. "Come now, therefore, and I will send you to Pharaoh that you may bring My people, the children of Israel, out of Egypt.""-Exodus 3:10. Moses said, ..."Who am I that I should go to Pharaoh, and that I should bring the children of Israel out of Egypt?""-Exodus 3:11.

God: ..."I will certainly be with you. And this shall be a sign to you that I have sent you: When you have brought the people out of Egypt, you shall serve God on this mountain.""-Exodus 3:12. Throughout Moses' leadership God never left him. He protected him from the beginning till the day he died. He experienced God in a tangible way as he spoke to Him face to face at times. "And it came to pass, when Moses entered the tabernacle, that the pillar of cloud descended and stood at the door of the tabernacle, and the LORD talked with Moses....So the LORD spoke to Moses face to face, as a man speaks to his friend. And he would return to the camp, ..."Exodus 33:9, 11a.

Joshua's security details

Joshua was Moses' servant who served God and Moses faithfully. God inaugurated him as the next leader to take over from Moses. Let us look at his security details, as he was about to step into the shoes of Moses as God's chosen leader of His people.

First of all, God reminds Joshua that Moses was dead and He God was all He had. He gave Joshua the instructions for the pending assignment. "After the death of Moses the servant of the LORD, it came to pass that the LORD spoke to Joshua the son of Nun, Moses' assistant, saying: "Moses My servant is dead. Now therefore, arise, go over this Jordan, you and all this people, to the land which I am giving to them—the children of Israel."-Joshua 1:1-2.

Now let's look at the words that invigorated Joshua. "No man shall be able to stand before you all the days of your life; as I was with Moses, so I will be with you. I will not leave you nor forsake you....Have I not commanded you? Be strong and of good courage; do not be afraid, nor be dismayed, for the LORD your God is with you wherever you go.""-Joshua 1:5, 9.

God protected Joshua throughout his leadership just as He promised. No nation was able to stand him until he died. The people served God all the days of Joshua without the same level of rebellion demonstrated during Moses' time. The people even served God after his death. "Israel served the LORD all the days of Joshua, and all the days of the elders who outlived Joshua, who had known all the works of the LORD which He had done for Israel."-Joshua 24:31.

Typical example: Elisha and the Syrian army. God opened the eyes of Elisha's servant upon the prophet's request. This was what happened before this event. The king of Syria declared war against God's children Israel at the time of the prophet Elisha. The king was not happy with his generals, as all their planned strategies seem to be known by Israel. Israel seems to be one step ahead of him. Whatever strategy planned by the Syrian army was revealed to Elisha who forewarn the king of Israel

The king of Syria called them and asked the traitor leaking information to Israel to own up. One servant gave him this information: "And the man of God sent to the king of Israel, saying, "Beware that you do not pass this place, for the Syrians are coming down there." And one of his servants said, "None, my lord, O king; but Elisha, the prophet who is in Israel, tells the king of Israel the words that you speak in your bedroom." So he said, "Go and see where he is, that I may send and get him." And it was told him, saying, "Surely he is in Dothan.""-II Kings 6:9, 12-13.

It was settled then! The king now commands his army to go and get Elisha. Let's look at the dramatic scenario.

Syrian army: "Therefore he sent horses and chariots and a great army there, and they came by night and surrounded the city."-II Kings 6:14. The city was surrounded and appeared to have been caught off guard.

In the morning Elisha's servant went out and saw their city besieged!

Servant of Elisha: "And when the servant of the man of God arose early and went out, there was an army, surrounding the city with horses and chariots. And his servant said to him, "Alas, my master! What shall we do?""-II Kings 6:15.

He was panicking and asked the prophet what should they do. The danger was real and there was nowhere to escape. Sometimes we need to remember God's track record of great miracles He had done in our lives before. If He did it then He can do it again. He delivered the whole nation under Moses when they faced the red see with the Egyptian army pursuing them.

Prophet Elisha: "So he answered, "Do not fear, for those who are with us are more than those who are with them.""-II Kings 6:16. Elisha prayed for God to open his eyes to see what he just said about those with them being more than the enemy's army.

God: "And Elisha prayed, and said, " LORD, I pray, open his eyes that he may see." Then the LORD opened the eyes of the young man, and he saw. And behold, the mountain was full of horses and chariots of fire all around Elisha."-II Kings 6:17.

Chariots of fire around Elisha!!The fact that we do not see our security details does not mean it doesn't exist. It is fully operational and ultimately powerful from heaven. Elisha knew about it and was not afraid of the thousands of enemy's army coming for him.
"So when the Syrians came down to him, Elisha prayed to the LORD, and said, "Strike this people, I pray, with blindness." And He struck them with blindness according to the word of Elisha."-   II Kings 6:18.

Just see the ease at which Elisha pray with absolute faith and authority and see how that was rewarded? He was a child and prophet of God. God's eyes were on Him and with His prophet under threat from the enemy; He would answer him to God's own glory. This is what Elisha said to the army when they came near to him blinded. "Now Elisha said to them, "This is not the way, nor is this the city. Follow me, and I will bring you to the man whom you seek." But he led them to Samaria."- II Kings 6:19.

This could have been a form blindness that caused Elisha to be shielded from the enemies so that they couldn't recognise him. Notice that they followed him when he offered to take them to the person they were looking for. "So it was, when they had come to Samaria, that Elisha said, " LORD, open the eyes of these men, that they may see." And the LORD opened their eyes, and they saw; and there they were, inside Samaria! Now when the king of Israel saw them, he said to Elisha, "My father, shall I kill them? Shall I kill them? ""-II Kings 6:20-21. Who can blame the king? How many times do you see your enemies led straight up to you blinded and helpless?

By opening their eyes to see where they were was embarrassing enough. The mighty army just realised that they were in the middle of Samaria. Elisha advised the sling not to kill then but be hospitable to them. "But he answered, "You shall not kill them. Would you kill those whom you have taken captive with your sword and your bow? Set food and water before them, that they may eat and drink and go to their master." Then he prepared a great feast for them; and after they ate and drank, he sent them away and they went to their master. So the bands of Syrian raiders came no more into the land of Israel."-II Kings 6:22-23.

Summary

- God is always with us and will never leave nor forsake us.

- Those heavenly secret agents protect us when our eyes are opened to their supernatural presence.

- The fact that we don't see our security details that does mean non-existent.

- You can ask God to open your eyes to see His impressive security forces surrounding you.

Chapter Six

God of Unlimited resources

Daniel's security details

Daniel was one of the captives from Israel who the king made a governor of one of his provinces. That was a prestigious position next to being a prime minister in our current political era. King Darius set up what was known as satrap who were to report to the governors. There were one hundred and twenty satraps and three governors.

Daniel, a foreign captive was appointed as one of the three governors! Daniel did not stop worshipping Almighty God in this foreign land that only worshiped Idols. Daniel was doing very well as a governor, which obviously attracted envy and hatred from some. "Then this Daniel distinguished himself above the governors and satraps, because an excellent spirit was in him; and the king gave thought to setting him over the whole realm." -Daniel 6:3.

Obviously the king planning to make him leader over the whole kingdom attracted the wrong crowd of haters. They plotted against Daniel. They could not find anything to accuse him of except his spiritual discipline. "Then these men said, "We shall not find any charge against this Daniel unless we find it against him concerning the law of his God.""-Daniel 6:5.

The other governors and satraps suggested to king Darius that a decree should be signed making all forms of worshipping other gods prohibited except to worship him. The king who did not know it was a plot against Daniel agreed and signed it into law.

Anyone who was found guilty will be thrown into the lion's den. "Now, O king, establish the decree and sign the writing, so that it cannot be changed, according to the law of the Medes and Persians, which does not alter." Therefore King Darius signed the written decree."-Daniel 6:8-9.

Daniel did not allow fear to prevent him from seeking the face of God and praying to Him. "Now when Daniel knew that the writing was signed, he went home. And in his upper room, with his windows open toward Jerusalem, he knelt down on his knees three times that day, and prayed and gave thanks before his God, as was his custom since early days. Then these men assembled and found Daniel praying and making supplication before his God."-Daniel 6:10-11.

The people went to the king and reported him, they referred to him as a captive and not the governor appointed by the king. Racism and the likes has been a human problem influenced by Satan and rooted in hatred. "So they answered and said before the king, "That Daniel, who is one of the captives from Judah, does not show due regard for you, O king, or for the decree that you have signed, but makes his petition three times a day.""-Daniel 6:13.

The king regretted his decision and tried to save Daniel. As the law had been passed Daniel had to put in the lions den. The king appeared to have believed that Daniel's God was able to save him. He spoke to Daniel before he was taken to the den.

"And the king, when he heard these words, was greatly displeased with himself, and set his heart on Daniel to deliver him; and he laboured till the going down of the sun to deliver him....So the king gave the command, and they brought Daniel and cast him into the den of lions. But the king spoke, saying to Daniel, "Your God, whom you serve continually, He will deliver you.""-Daniel 6:14, 16.

The king refused any entertainment and couldn't sleep but rather fasted. Early morning he went to the entrance of the lion's den and called Daniel as a servant of the living God. "Now the king went to his palace and spent the night fasting; and no musicians were brought before him. Also his sleep went from him. Then the king arose very early in the morning and went in haste to the den of lions. And when he came to the den, he cried out with a lamenting voice to Daniel. The king spoke, saying to Daniel, "Daniel, servant of the living God, has your God, whom you serve continually, been able to deliver you from the lions?""-Daniel 6:18-20.

Daniel responded to the delight of the king to know that he was alive. Daniel's security details covered this and his accusers influenced by Satan's spirit did not prevail.

This was Daniel's own words: "My God sent His angel and shut the lions' mouths, so that they have not hurt me, because I was found innocent before Him; and also, O king, I have done no wrong before you.""-Daniel 6:22. The king was overjoyed and commanded him to be brought out. "Now the king was exceedingly glad for him, and commanded that they should take Daniel up out of the den. So Daniel was taken up out of the den, and no injury whatever was found on him, because he believed in his God."-Daniel 6:23.

The people who allow Satan to use as accusers doing his dirty work will not go unpunished. They will surely face the consequences of plotting and hurting God's children using their lifestyle or faithfulness to God as the basis for their hurt. "And the king gave the command, and they brought those men who had accused Daniel, and they cast them into the den of lions—them, their children, and their wives; and the lions overpowered them, and broke all their bones in pieces before they ever came to the bottom of the den."-Daniel 6:24. The king praised this awesome God of Daniel.

"Then King Darius wrote: To all peoples, nations, and languages that dwell in all the earth: Peace be multiplied to you. I make a decree that in every dominion of my kingdom men must tremble and fear before the God of Daniel. For He is the living God, and steadfast forever; His kingdom is the one, which shall not be destroyed, and His dominion shall endure to the end. He delivers and rescues, and He works signs and wonders in heaven and on earth, Who has delivered Daniel from the power of the lions. So this Daniel prospered in the reign of Darius and in the reign of Cyrus the Persian."-Daniel 6:25-28

Summary

- Satan may influence people to plot evil, lies and accusations against you. However they will find out that the basis for that lies was only to do with your faithful walk with Jesus Christ.
- Always remember that no matter how difficult the trial you can endure because God is with you.
- God never leave nor forsake you even if the situation is of this unbelievable magnitude. He is bigger and greater than any problem.
- You can never be killed if God does not allow that to happen.
- He will always elevate and honour your steadfast love for Him.

Chapter Seven

Jesus security details

Baby Jesus security details

Jesus Christ had to be born as a child under the Law of Moses and the law of sin and death to redeem Adam's entire race. He carried all the purpose of God for this salvation in Him. The angels who broke the news confirmed this. It was not a secret. Satan knew the Messiah has been born and influenced the authorities to try and kill him by killing all children less than two years born around his time.

When that law was passed, the Baby Saviour's security details covered that too. Angels were at His disposal right from the time of announcing His conception and birth. They were at His disposal to move Him away from harm when the king was looking to destroy Him.

What happened was that wise men followed Jesus' special star to the place where baby Jesus was born. Before they got to where the baby King was born, they first made enquires in Jerusalem and that got to the king, Herod. "Now after Jesus was born in Bethlehem of Judea in the days of Herod the king, behold, wise men from the East came to Jerusalem, saying, "Where is He who has been born King of the Jews? For we have seen His star in the East and have come to worship Him.""-Matthew 2:1-2.

Somehow this grown up king was disturbed about a new Baby King who has been born. He called the priest and experts to ask where the Christ was to be born. They told him and he hatched a secret plan to kill the baby. If this was not satanic influenced then what else was controlling Herod's mind? "And when he had gathered all the chief priests and scribes of the people together, he inquired of them where the Christ was to be born. So they said to him, "In Bethlehem of Judea, for thus it is written by the prophet: 'But you, Bethlehem, in the land of Judah, Are not the least among the rulers of Judah; For out of you shall come a Ruler Who will shepherd My people Israel.' ""-Matthew 2:4-6.

The king called the wise men secretly and asked them to go and search for the baby in Bethlehem and afterwards come back with information to him so he will also go and worship Him. Sounded very decent and humbling. Was that king Herod's intention? "And he sent them to Bethlehem and said, "Go and search carefully for the young Child, and when you have found Him, bring back word to me, that I may come and worship Him also.""-Matthew 2:8.

The wise men went to Bethlehem, found the baby King presented gifts and worshiped Him. "When they saw the star, they rejoiced with exceedingly great joy. And when they had come into the house, they saw the young Child with Mary His mother, and fell down and worshiped Him. And when they had opened their treasures, they presented gifts to Him: gold, frankincense, and myrrh."-Matthew 2:10-11.

Intelligence information

We have been studying on various ways that God writes and execute our security details. One of the important works of the secret service is always looking out for intelligence information to make vital security decisions. We are fortunate enough to have God who knows and sees everything and everyone's intentions!

God saw what Herod's intentions were and acted. "Then, being divinely warned in a dream that they should not return to Herod, they departed for their own country another way."-Matthew 2:12.

God sent an angel to secure the Baby Jesus and His earthly parents. "Now when they had departed, behold, an angel of the Lord appeared to Joseph in a dream, saying, "Arise, take the young Child and His mother, flee to Egypt, and stay there until I bring you word; for Herod will seek the young Child to destroy Him.""-Matthew 2:13.

Herod did not take it lightly and went into 'satanic beast mode.' "Then Herod, when he saw that he was deceived by the wise men, was exceedingly angry; and he sent forth and put to death all the male children who were in Bethlehem and in all its districts, from two years old and under, according to the time which he had determined from the wise men."-Matthew 2:16.

"Now when Herod was dead, behold, an angel of the Lord appeared in a dream to Joseph in Egypt, saying, "Arise, take the young Child and His mother, and go to the land of Israel, for those who sought the young Child's life are dead." Then he arose, took the young Child and His mother, and came into the land of Israel."-Matthew 2:19-21.

Adult Jesus security details

Temptation: For Jesus to redeem Adam's race from the curse of sin and death, He had to go through some series of real life experiences in order to fulfill His purpose of saving us. One of the main experiences was the three fold temptation Satan used to carefully lure Adam and Eve to choose to sin against God Almighty.

The Holy Spirit took Jesus to the wilderness to be tempted by Satan. This happened and Jesus used the Word to defeat Satan three times. Afterwards the angels came back to minister to Him. Jesus' security details were always intact apart from occasional withdrawals to ensure other experiences and tests takes place. "Then the devil left Him, and behold, angels came and ministered to Him."-Matthew 4:11.

First sermon and security details

At the start of His ministry, Jesus went to the synagogue and as His custom was, they handed Him a scroll to read. "And He was handed the book of the prophet Isaiah. And when He had opened the book, He found the place where it was written:
""The Spirit of the LORD is upon Me, Because He has anointed Me To preach the gospel to the poor; He has sent Me to heal the brokenhearted, To proclaim liberty to the captives And recovery of sight to the blind, To set at liberty those who are oppressed; To proclaim the acceptable year of the LORD.""-Luke 4:17-19. Once He finished reading, He closed it and said something very important and truthful, but at the same time one that enraged the people because of the meaning and significance.

"And He began to say to them, "Today this Scripture is fulfilled in your hearing.""-Luke 4:21. Now the people who had come to the synagogue to worship were enraged because Jesus' teaching after reading that scripture implied that He was the Messiah! "So all those in the synagogue, when they heard these things, were filled with wrath, and rose up and thrust Him out of the city; and they led Him to the brow of the hill on which their city was built, that they might throw Him down over the cliff. Then passing through the midst of them, He went His way."-Luke 4:28-30.

Do you know what kinds of violence human rage can cause? It can carry out evil right up to murder. They were about to throw Jesus, the Messiah Who just introduced His ministry, down the mountain on which the temple was built. Due to His security details, no one was able to touch Him. Jesus had not given permission to be killed, as it was not the right time. Jesus walked through the midst of them and went His way. What powerful form of protection!

Security during preparation for death and resurrection: Fast forward to the last days of Jesus fulfilling His mission of saving humanity. Jesus had gone to the garden of Gethsemane to pray. The weight of our sins and the intensity of it weighed heavily on Jesus to the extent that He asked the Father to take it away if possible. If it wasn't then He will fulfill the Father's will as always…"saying, "Father, if it is Your will, take this cup away from Me; nevertheless not My will, but Yours, be done." Then an angel appeared to Him from heaven, strengthening Him. And being in agony, He prayed more earnestly. Then His sweat became like great drops of blood falling down to the ground."-Luke 22:42-44.

Notice that an angel came from Heaven to strengthen Him. Are you feeling so week under the strain of what you are allowed to go through as part of your calling that you wish to give up? Speak to God and He will send an angel to come and strengthen you!

In the garden of Gethsemane, Jesus took three of His closest friends to go and pray with Him as He was about to carry in Himself all the sins of the world and be mistreated by sinners right up to His crucifixion. On human level this was not an easy task for Jesus to face while He was praying to the Father. After His prayers it was time for Judas, one of His disciples to come with His enemies to betray Him.

Judas came to fulfill his promise to the high priest after asking for those 30 pieces of silver to betray Jesus. During this time somehow some of the disciples thought they could fight the total enemies with a mini sword! One of the disciples actually cut off the ear of one of the servant of the priest's. Jesus was not pleased with that at all.

"But Jesus said to him, "Put your sword in its place, for all who take the sword will perish by the sword. Or do you think that I cannot now pray to My Father, and He will provide Me with more than twelve legions of angels? How then could the Scriptures be fulfilled, that it must happen thus?""- Matthew 26:52-54.

During the time of Jesus, the standard legion of Roman soldiers consisted of about 6000 men. These were not ordinary soldiers but the elite soldiers of the Roman army. Jesus had access to over twelve legions of angels at His disposal as part of His security details. He could have prayed and they would be there before anyone could blink! Well, let's do some mathematical calculations here:

1 legion of angels = 6000 angels (minimum)
Therefore 12 legion=6000 X 12= 72, 000.

Jesus had over 72,000 angels ready to do anything He asked on the night of His unlawful arrest. This means all the angels were at His disposal. Let us look at what kind of power these angels have by looking at the details of Hezekiah.

Hezekiah's security details
Strength of ministering angels Story.
Sennacherib was a powerful king of Assyria at the of king Hezekiah of Israel. Hezekiah was the king of God's people. Sennacherib planned to destroy God's people Israel and was boasting against the Lord God.

Basically he said no one could deliver any nation he attacked from his hands. "Then the Rabshakeh said to them, "Say now to Hezekiah, 'Thus says the great king, the king of Assyria: "What confidence is this in which you trust? I say you speak of having plans and power for war; but they are mere words. Now in whom do you trust, that you rebel against me?..."But if you say to me, 'We trust in the LORD our God,' is it not He whose high places and whose altars Hezekiah has taken away, and said to Judah and Jerusalem, 'You shall worship before this altar'?" '"-Isaiah 36:4-5, 7.

This was the boasting that was about to cost him dearly as he did not know the security God's people had.

"Beware lest Hezekiah persuade you, saying, "The LORD will deliver us." Has any one of the gods of the nations delivered its land from the hand of the king of Assyria? Where are the gods of Hamath and Arpad? Where are the gods of Sepharvaim? Indeed, have they delivered Samaria from my hand? Who among all the gods of these lands have delivered their countries from my hand, that the LORD should deliver Jerusalem from my hand?' ""-Isaiah 36:18-20. He was comparing the Almighty God with familiar spirits parading as gods!

The words of this king were sent to king Hezekiah who passed it on to the prophet Isaiah for the Lord's response. The prophet sent the word of the Lord to the king. "And Isaiah said to them, "Thus you shall say to your master, 'Thus says the LORD: "Do not be afraid of the words which you have heard, with which the servants of the king of Assyria have blasphemed Me."-Isaiah 37:6. "Surely I will send a spirit upon him, and he shall hear a rumour and return to his own land; and I will cause him to fall by the sword in his own land." -Isaiah 37:7.

God's answers

God said because Hezekiah prayed Sennacherib was not going to step a foot in Israel and not a single arrow was to be shot. God was going to defend His own city. ""Therefore thus says the LORD concerning the king of Assyria: 'He shall not come into this city, nor shoot an arrow there, nor come before it with shield, nor build a siege mound against it. By the way that he came, by the same shall he return; and he shall not come into this city,' Says the LORD. 'For I will defend this city, to save it For My own sake and for My servant David's sake.' ""-Isaiah 37:33-35.

What happened next will give us an idea what angels can do when given the orders on our behalf. "Then the angel of the LORD went out, and killed in the camp of the Assyrians one hundred and eighty-five thousand; and when people arose early in the morning, there were the corpses—all dead."-Isaiah 37:36.

One angel killed 185,000 enemy soldiers! Sennacherib went back to his country and as he was worshiping his idol, two of his sons killed him.

Let's add this new figures to what we started. If 1 angel has got the power to kill 185,000 how many can the combined power of a legion of angels kill?

1= 185,000
6000=1,110,000,000. Which are 1 billion, one hundred and ten million men!
Now let's multiply 12 legions by 185,000.
That equals to 13,320,000,000. That is a whooping 13 billion plus people! The year is 2020 and the world's population is just over 7 billion.

The angels available during the time of Jesus' arrest could have killed the entire population of our time almost twice over! That is the security details we have as children of God. Take a few moment and let this truth sink into your spirit. If you are finding it difficult to believe this have a look at how God has positioned all those who have accepted Jesus Christ as their Saviour. Let this comfort you:

"For as many as are led by the Spirit of God, these are sons of God. For you did not receive the spirit of bondage again to fear, but you received the Spirit of adoption by whom we cry out, "Abba, Father." The Spirit Himself bears witness with our spirit that we are children of God, and if children, then heirs—heirs of God and joint heirs with Christ, if indeed we suffer with Him, that we may also be glorified together."- Romans 8:14-17.

Summary

- Do you rejoice by knowing that God protected Baby Jesus to ensure He fulfilled the purpose of saving all including yourself?

- That was an example to us on what He does for us.

- Accusations and Satan's false witnesses do not change God's truth and power to protect us.

- The more the evil against you the more God's protective hand is released on your behalf.

Chapter Eight

Peter's security details

Restored back

Although Jesus' prediction of Peter denying knowing Him three times happened, he was totally restored after Jesus resurrected from the dead. This happened at the seashore. Peter and the rest of the disciples went fishing and came back to shore without catching anything. This was after Jesus had resurrected from the dead as promised.

Jesus was standing at the shore. When they returned He asked them if they caught anything. This is what He said to them and the results thereof. "Children, have you any food?" They answered Him, "No." And He said to them, "Cast the net on the right side of the boat, and you will find some. " So they cast, and now they were not able to draw it in because of the multitude of fish."-John 21:5-6.

One of the disciples then recognised the Messiah in His post resurrection glorious and powerful body and countenance.

Once Peter heard about the Lord he hurried to get to Him. Jesus had already prepared breakfast for them. "Therefore that disciple whom Jesus loved said to Peter, "It is the Lord!" Now when Simon Peter heard that it was the Lord, he put on his outer garment (for he had removed it), and plunged into the sea....Then, as soon as they had come to land, they saw a fire of coals there, and fish laid on it, and bread. Jesus said to them, "Bring some of the fish which you have just caught.""-John 21:7, 9-10.

No one asked Jesus who He was. "Simon Peter went up and dragged the net to land, full of large fish, one hundred and fifty-three; and although there were so many, the net was not broken. Jesus said to them, "Come and eat breakfast." Yet none of the disciples dared ask Him, "Who are You?"—knowing that it was the Lord."-John 21:11-12.

It was on this occasion that Jesus restored Peter the same number of times He denied Him, which was three times. He asked if he loved Him. If so He commissioned him to feed His sheep. "So when they had eaten breakfast, Jesus said to Simon Peter, "Simon, son of Jonah, do you love Me more than these?" He said to Him, "Yes, Lord; You know that I love You." He said to him, "Feed My lambs.""-John 21:15.

Leadership and full security details

Immediately after Jesus' ascension into heaven, we see Peter taking on the lead to share the gospel of Jesus Christ without the Lord's physical presence. They were commanded by Jesus to wait in Jerusalem for the promise of the Holy Spirit, which was the Father's promise.

They did and the coming of the Holy Spirit was absolutely spectacular and ultimately powerful. The Holy Spirit gave people the power to speak in other languages that they did not understand praising God. "And suddenly there came a sound from heaven, as of a rushing mighty wind, and it filled the whole house where they were sitting. Then there appeared to them divided tongues, as of fire, and one sat upon each of them. And they were all filled with the Holy Spirit and began to speak with other tongues, as the Spirit gave them utterance."- Acts 2:2-4.

It happened that there were people from all over the world gathered at the same city. They heard these Jewish people in a room praising God Almighty in all their various languages. Some marveled while others said they were drunk. Peter came out and preached the first sermon without Jesus' physical presence." But Peter, standing up with the eleven, raised his voice and said to them, "Men of Judea and all who dwell in Jerusalem, let this be known to you, and heed my words. For these are not drunk, as you suppose, since it is only the third hour of the day ...'And it shall come to pass in the last days, says God, That I will pour out of My Spirit on all flesh;

Your sons and your daughters shall prophesy, Your young men shall see visions, Your old men shall dream dreams." Acts 2:14-15, 17.

Peter preached the whole gospel and the history behind the coming of the Holy Spirit that day as they just witnessed. ""Men of Israel, hear these words: Jesus of Nazareth, a Man attested by God to you by miracles, wonders, and signs which God did through Him in your midst, as you yourselves also know—"-Acts 2:22.

After the sermon many were convicted by the Holy Spirit and asked what to do in order to inherit eternal life. "And with many other words he testified and exhorted them, saying, "Be saved from this perverse generation." Then those who gladly received his word were baptised; and that day about three thousand souls were added to them."-Acts 2:40-41.

This significant miracle also attracted the authorities who murdered Jesus and hoped that was going to be over. Now He rose again from the dead, defied gravity and ascends to heaven with His name now working more miracles.

After this vital newly formed church growth, Peter and John going to the temple to pray saw a beggar strategically placed at the entrance to beg for alms. Peter spoke to him and said: "Then Peter said, "Silver and gold I do not have, but what I do have I give you: In the name of Jesus Christ of Nazareth, rise up and walk." And he took him by the right hand and lifted him up, and immediately his feet and anklebones received strength. So he, leaping up, stood and walked and entered the temple with them—walking, leaping, and praising God."-Acts 3:6-8.

The workings of miracles through the preaching of the gospel of Jesus Christ did not sit well with the priest, captain of the temple and the Sadducees. "being greatly disturbed that they taught the people and preached in Jesus the resurrection from the dead. And they laid hands on them, and put them in custody until the next day, for it was already evening."-Acts 4:2-3.

They refused to see the notable miracle that just happened because of their hatred for Jesus Christ. However many still believed after witnessing this awesome miracle. "However, many of those who heard the word believed; and the number of the men came to be about five thousand."-Acts 4:4.

The name of Jesus was banned. However Peter and the others continued preaching about Jesus the resurrection and power to save.

Security details for this level

Now that Peter was carrying out leadership role in leading the newly formed church, how was he protected? It was clear that he had attracted the attention of the same people who murdered the Messiah in the physical and unlawful sense. Let's look at one incident that tells of his security details.

"Now about that time Herod the king stretched out his hand to harass some from the church. Then he killed James the brother of John with the sword. And because he saw that it pleased the Jews, he proceeded further to seize Peter also. Now it was during the Days of Unleavened Bread."-Acts 12:1-3.

This was King Herod's security for this unarmed innocent follower of Christ and servant of the living God. "So when he had arrested him, he put him in prison, and delivered him to four squads of soldiers to keep him, intending to bring him before the people after Passover."-Acts 12:4.

 The congregation was praying for him. "And when Herod was about to bring him out, that night Peter was sleeping, bound with two chains between two soldiers; and the guards before the door were keeping the prison."-Acts 12:6. Something supernatural happened as God had commissioned Peter to be preaching the good news of the kingdom of God with signs and wonders following.

Heavenly security
Angel of God: "Now behold, an angel of the Lord stood by him, and a light shone in the prison; and he struck Peter on the side and raised him up, saying, "Arise quickly!" And his chains fell off his hands."-Acts 12:7

Angel of God: "Then the angel said to him, "Gird yourself and tie on your sandals"; and so he did. And he said to him, "Put on your garment and follow me.""-Acts 12:8.

The angel was waiting for this right time to show how God's children are secured when our time is not yet up to be called home. Peter had more work to do. Peter followed the angel past all the guards still thinking he was having a vision. "When they were past the first and the second guard posts, they came to the iron gate that leads to the city, which opened to them of its own accord; and they went out and went down one street, and immediately the angel departed from him."-Acts 12:10.

Once the angel brought Peter out of the prison which was injustice done to him, he departed. "And when Peter had come to himself, he said, "Now I know for certain that the Lord has sent His angel, and has delivered me from the hand of Herod and from all the expectation of the Jewish people." So, when he had considered this, he came to the house of Mary, the mother of John whose surname was Mark, where many were gathered together praying."-Acts 12:11-12.

The gospel cannot be imprisoned. The purpose of God for your life will not be put to shame or destroyed. God will preserve your life until He accomplishes all that He has purposed for you. What seem to have imprisoned your life because you live a peculiar life to please and honour God as a child of God? Once you get closer to God with the desire to share His gospel, then expect His security details for you to be that comprehensive and powerful just as the one given to Peter. Angels are still sent to minister and protect us. As long as we are preaching and sharing the life changing world-shaking gospel, angels on assignment will get us out of any satanic bondage.

Fortunately the spirit behind the prevention of the spreading of God's gospel will be dealt with. This means all those involved who have allowed themselves to be used, as agents will face various consequences such as Judas and Herod's death. "So on a set day Herod, arrayed in royal apparel, sat on his throne and gave an oration to them....Then immediately an angel of the Lord struck him, because he did not give glory to God. And he was eaten by worms and died. But the word of God grew and multiplied."-Acts 12:21, 23-24. What happened was that when he spoke the people said he was a god. He did not refute that causing his death.

Summary

- No matter how you have fallen away from Christ, He is able to restore and protect you again.

- The gospel of Christ Jesus that you are determined to share will attract Satan's wrath and things may seem unpleasant. However, God's security details remains robust.

- His angels are there for your protection. They are not diminished in numbers!

- God is able to punish those who hate Him and causes you pain because of your godly lifestyle.

❖**Chapter Nine**
Your security details In Christ

In Christ

For all of us who have chosen to accept Jesus Christ as our Lord and personal Saviour, our life is now in Christ.

Looking at what the apostle Peter attempted to do when Jesus allowed Himself to be arrested to voluntarily lay down His life for the sins of the human race, that was pointless. What was one little sword going to do against the armed men who came to arrest Jesus anyway? That was why Jesus had to teach him not to rely on human strength but in God's strength.

We are to understand the purposes for our life and the tests that come with it. Jesus knew that He was to voluntarily lay down His life for the sin of the human race at that particular time hence He chose not to deploy the legions of angels to wipe out the soldiers who came to arrest Him.

This is how we normally try to react and resolve issues using our flesh, carnal mind and methods. We look for solutions based on what we have available to us without consulting the highest authority that has been given to us. We studied how the servant of Elisha was overwhelmed when he saw the numerous army of the enemy surrounding his master. Instead of Elisha panicking, he was closer to God and could see the supernatural armies of God with him. This was so real that he asked God to open the eyes of his Servant to see as well.

We are totally secured in Gods protection. Just before Jesus finished the work of redemption, He prayed for all His disciples and one of the areas was our protection from Satan. "I do not pray that You should take them out of the world, but that You should keep them from the evil one. They are not of the world, just as I am not of the world."-John 17:15-16.

Before we argue that this prayer was for the immediate apostles, we should be rest assured that Jesus did not forget all those to come to Him afterwards. ""I do not pray for these alone, but also for those who will believe in Me through their word; that they all may be one, as You, Father, are in Me, and I in You; that they also may be one in Us, that the world may believe that You sent Me."-John 17:20-21.

Renew mindset

With all the areas we have studied, we are totally secured in God. He only take away some part of the security during testing times and that is not to punish us but to promote us to higher levels with greater security details as we saw with Job in particular. We saw that evident in Jesus Christ as well. This chapter is for you to prayerfully reflect on all the protection you have in God and times He boast about you.

"Many are the afflictions of the righteous, but the LORD delivers him out of them all."-Psalms 34:19.

We will be exposed and allowed to face trials, tests and afflictions. As painful as these may be, know for sure that Jesus will not leave nor forsake us. He wants us to have endurance that helps us to mature in Him by developing our faith to the highest level. One thing I will encourage us is this, Jesus has the power to fix any problems we will ever come across on earth. We should always keep this in mind.

As we learnt from Peter's situation, we should not jump in and make things worse by taking matters into our hands. This means that whenever we are faced with problems we should take a moment and remind ourselves that Jesus can handle the problem without our intervention. We should think about that first before we attempt to 'swing the sword' like Peter did.

What I studied and continue to do is to pray and ask Jesus what I am supposed to do and wait for the answer. I then follow the instructions given to me from His answer. And yes He does answer and His supernatural power is simply unbelievable and amazing. Rather than my sword swinging unwisely, His supernatural power swings into action to solve every impossible dilemma I face! He is able to do the same for you.

We are joint heirs with Jesus Christ and have access to the resources of Gods kingdom. Angels are at our disposal as well. Ask God to open your eyes to see. He that is with you is greater than your enemies surrounding you.

Reference

1. "Secret Service Fast Facts". *CNN*. May 3, 2019. Retrieved June 3, 2019.
2. Chicago Bible Student. February 6, 2016. " Did Job live before Abraham or before Noah?"
    https://chicagobible.org/did-job-live-before-abraham-or-before-noah/
3. renner.org. Twelve legions of angels. April 11, 2016. https://renner.org/twelve-legions-of-angels/

www.ingramcontent.com/pod-product-compliance
Lightning Source LLC
Chambersburg PA
CBHW051344150726
48000CB00003B/1043